SHREWSBURY TO CREWE

Vic Mitchell and Keith Smith

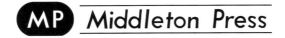

Front cover: A long distance express speeds through Wrenbury, hauled by 4-6-2 no. 45592 in May 1962. One young spotter and an elderly oil lamp add to the period atmosphere. (Colour-Rail.com)

Back cover upper: It is 28th May 1939 and GWR 2-6-2T no. 5165 waits to depart from Nantwich, probably the busiest station on the route. The sign offers a choice of six destinations from here. (Bentley coll.)

Back cover lower: Leaving Crewe on 29th March 1980 is Type 2 diesel no. 25224, with its steam heating boiler blowing off. It is heading the 12.22 to Cardiff, which will run via Shrewsbury. (P.Jones)

Published September 2013

ISBN 978 1 908174 48 2

© Middleton Press, 2013

Design Deborah Esher
Typesetting Barbara Mitchell

Published by
>   *Middleton Press*
>   *Easebourne Lane*
>   *Midhurst*
>   *West Sussex*
>   *GU29 9AZ*
Tel: 01730 813169
Fax: 01730 812601
Email: info@middletonpress.co.uk
www.middletonpress.co.uk

Printed in the United Kingdom by Henry Ling Limited, at the Dorset Press, Dorchester, DT1 1HD

INDEX

ACKNOWLEDGEMENTS

We are very grateful for the assistance received from many of those mentioned in the credits, also to A.R.Carder, A.J.Castledine, G.Croughton, D.A.Johnson, N.Langridge, B.Lewis, J.P.McCrickard, Mr D. and Dr S.Salter, T.Walsh and in particular, our always supportive wives, Barbara Mitchell and Janet Smith.

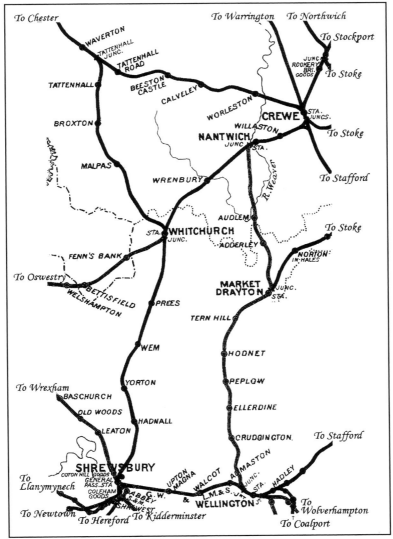

Railway Clearing House map for 1947.

GEOGRAPHICAL SETTING

We start close to the River Severn and the ancient castle in the historic market town of Shrewsbury. There is a steady climb for three miles out of the deep valley and at Wem the route passes over the east flowing River Roden.

An undulating and fairly straight course follows over high ground, largely devoid of trees, to reach Whitchurch. Here the line serving Malpas and Tattenhall diverged and ran north, only a few miles from the Welsh border.

A steady descent to Nantwich follows, where the River Weaver is bridged. The remainder of the route to Crewe is now largely urbanised. The line was built mostly in Shropshire, passing into Cheshire north of Whitchurch. The final miles are on the Cheshire Plain. The route traverses red sandstones and mudstones, with lias clay between Wem and Whitchurch.

The maps are to the scale of 25ins to 1 mile, with north at the top unless otherwise indicated.

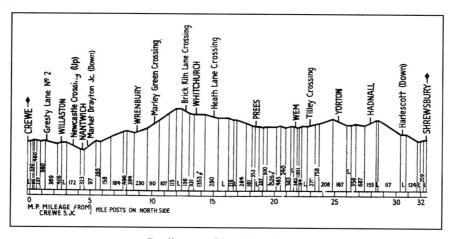

Gradient profile with mileage.

HISTORICAL BACKGROUND

The first line in the area was that of the Grand Junction Railway, which linked Birmingham and Liverpool in 1837. There followed branches from Crewe to Chester in 1840 and from Crewe to Stockport in 1842.

Shrewsbury received trains from Chester in 1848, from Wellington in 1849, from Ludlow in 1852, from Welshpool in 1861, from Bridgnorth in 1862 and from Llanymynech in 1866.

Shrewsbury and Crewe were linked by the London & North Western Railway on 1st September 1858, via Whitchurch. This was served by a line from Ellesmere from 1863, the route soon becoming part of the Cambrian Railways and eventually the Great Western Railway, in 1922. The GJR had formed part of the LNWR in 1846.

The LNWR opened the route northwest from Whitchurch to its Chester line on 1st October 1872. The link lost its passenger service on 16th September 1957 and closed completely in 1964.

The grouping of 1923 brought the LNWR into the London Midland & Scottish Railway, which became the London Midland Region of British Railways upon nationalisation in 1948. The route of this album was operated by Wales & West upon privatisation, the franchise starting on 13th October 1996 and lasting until 7th December 2003, when Arriva Trains Wales took over.

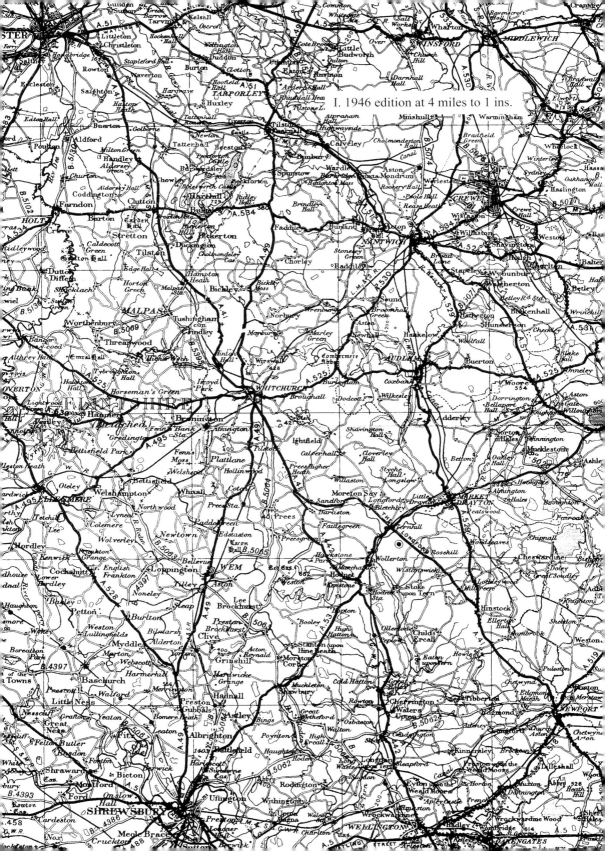

I. 1946 edition at 4 miles to 1 ins.

PASSENGER SERVICES

The table below indicates the number of local trains on both routes, but excludes trains running on less than five days per week and long distance ones not calling at intermediate stations. Many of these have operated between Cardiff and Manchester and/or Liverpool. In the 21st century, most ran between the first two cities, but called at all stops on the route.

	via NANTWICH		via TATTENHALL	
	Weekdays	Sundays	Weekdays	Sundays
1860	7	1	-	-
1873	5	2	5	0
1902	9	2	5	0
1930	10	3	8	0
1952	7	5	5	0
1987	9	3	-	-
2013	13	5	-	-

Between the wars, one or two long distance trains carried restaurant cars and ran daily. Some had through coaches between West Wales and Scotland, while others had through coaches to Birkenhead, via Malpas. In recent years, DMUs have run over the route, while working between Milford Haven and Manchester.

December 1873

CREWE, NANTWICH, WHITCHURCH, WEM, and SHREWSBURY.—L. & N. W. [District Man., Ephraim Wood.

June 1869

WHITCHURCH, TATTENHALL, and CHESTER.

NOTES.

E or Ɇ Except Saturdays
S Saturdays only.

November 1930

Table 90   CHESTER, TATTENHALL, and WHITCHURCH

E Except Saturdays.   S Saturdays only.   U Wednesdays only   X Except Wednesdays and Saturdays.
Z Through Carriages to Shrewsbury (Table 87)

September 1952

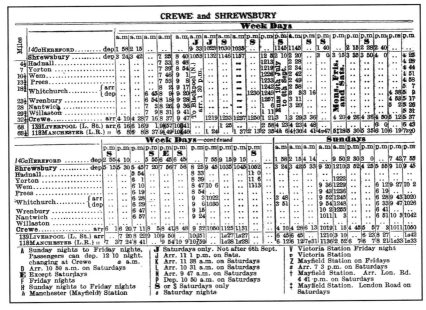

CREWE and SHREWSBURY

A Sunday nights to Friday nights,
   Passengers can dep. 12 10 night,
   changing at Crewe   a a.m.
D Arr. 10 50 a.m. on Saturdays
E Except Saturdays
F Friday nights
H Sunday nights to Friday nights
h Manchester (Mayfield) Station.
J Saturdays only. Not after 6th Sept.
K Arr. 11 1 p.m. on Sats.
L Arr. 11 38 a.m. on Saturdays
M Arr. 10 31 a.m. on Saturdays
N Arr. 9 47 a.m. on Saturdays
P Dep. 10 50 a.m. on Saturdays
S or Ṣ Saturdays only
s Saturday nights
V Victoria Station Friday night
v Victoria Station
Z Mayfield Station on Fridays
† Mayfield Station. Arr. Lon. Rd.
   4 41 p.m. on Saturdays
‡ Mayfield Station. London Road on
   Saturdays

September 1952

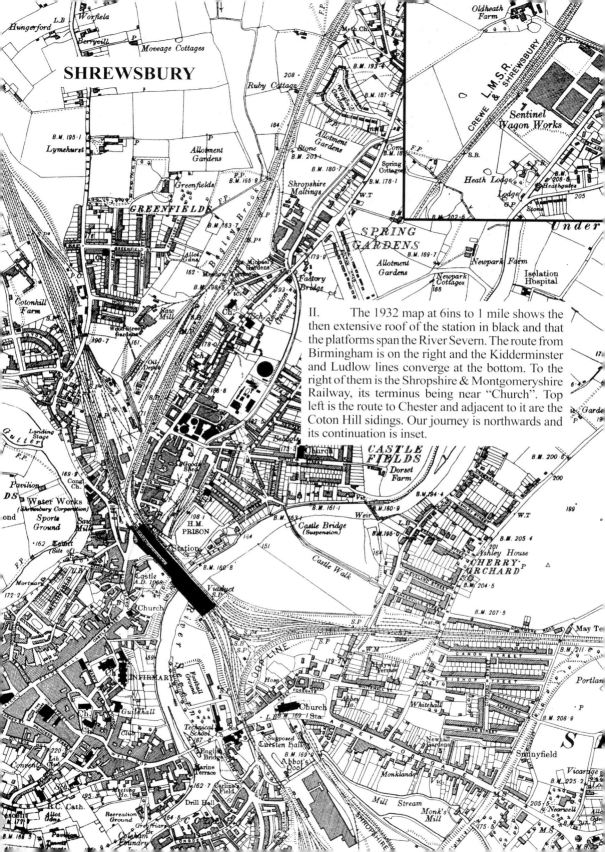

II.   The 1932 map at 6ins to 1 mile shows the then extensive roof of the station in black and that the platforms span the River Severn. The route from Birmingham is on the right and the Kidderminster and Ludlow lines converge at the bottom. To the right of them is the Shropshire & Montgomeryshire Railway, its terminus being near "Church". Top left is the route to Chester and adjacent to it are the Coton Hill sidings. Our journey is northwards and its continuation is inset.

1.	The station was constructed jointly by the first two users, in a style to complement the adjacent castle. However, the part on the left was added in 1854 and major platform alterations took place in 1861 to 1863. The building initially appeared to have only two storeys, but in 1900 to 1901 the approach was lowered, the cellars were exposed and windows were fitted therein. (R.M.Casserley coll.)

2.	This is the wreckage of an LNWR express at the north end of the station on 15th October 1907. The derailment resulted in the loss of 18 lives. The photograph is from the tower of the Perseverance Iron Works and features Crewe Junction Box. (D.Bannocks coll.)

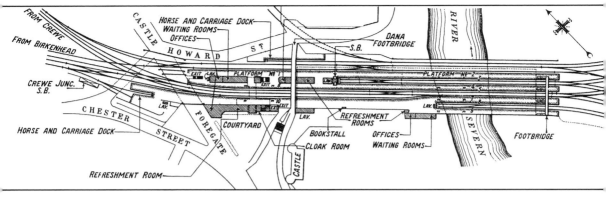

III. This 1932 diagram shows the platform numbering in use until 1950. The two tracks at the top curve to the Shropshire Union goods yard, which met the canal of that name. This ran north, under Factory Bridge, and served the gasworks, the holder of which is shown as a black circle on map II. (Railway Magazine)

3. The exterior view in 1948 includes the footbridge, which was provided to link the platforms and serve a public footpath. Until the entrance was lowered, and a subway was created, everyone had to cross the tracks on the level. (R.M.Casserley coll.)

4. Ex-LMS class 4P 2-6-4T no. 40235 partly obscures ex-GWR "Castle" class 4-6-0 no. 5033 *Broughton Castle*, soon after the formation of BR. This brought an end to joint ownership of the station. Removal of the extensive roof was completed in 1963. The northern part had been dismantled in 1931 to 1932. (Unknown)

5. We look south from the footbridge in the early 1960s and gain a rare glimpse of the crossover and the connection to the Shropshire Union goods yard on the left. It closed on 5th April 1971 and is shown on map II. (Unknown)

6.   The ex-LNWR Crewe Junction signal box of 1903 is seen in about 1953. It was fitted with 120 levers and was still in use in 2013. Central Box was north of the two bays from 1904 until 1961. It was built by the LNWR with 69 levers and the crossover seen in picture 5 was controlled by it. (P.J.Garland/R.S.Carpenter)

For other views of this area, please see:
Branch Line to Shrewsbury (The S&MR)
Shrewsbury to Chester
Shrewsbury to Newtown
Shrewsbury to Ludlow
Wolverhampton to Shrewsbury
Kidderminster to Shrewsbury

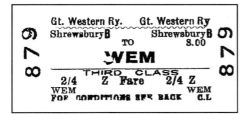

Gt. Western Ry.   Gt. Western Ry
Shrewsbury B   Shrewsbury B
            TO   8.00
879   879
8   WEM   8
7   THIRD CLASS   7
9   2/4   Z Fare   2/4 Z   9
        WEM   WEM
        FOR CONDITIONS SEE BACK C.L

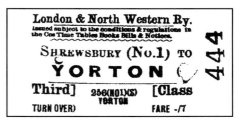

London & North Western Ry.
Issued subject to the conditions & regulations in
the Cos Time Tables Books Bills & Notices.
SHREWSBURY (No.1) TO
444   444
        YORTON
Third]   256(NO1)(S)   [Class
             YORTON
TURN OVER)   FARE -/7

7.   The curves for trains arriving from Crewe are seen from the platform ramp at about the same time. The building housed the offices of the former GWR's Castle Gate goods yard, which lasted until about 1980. (P.J.Garland/R.S.Carpenter)

8.   The signals on the left of the previous picture are on the right of this one, which is from the same era. The two goods sheds are shown on the map. (Milepost 92½)

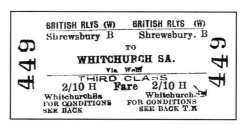

9.   The castle is top right as a train leaves for Chester in the early 1960s, hauled by no. 4954 *Plaish Hall*. On the right is "Royal Scot" class 4-6-0 no. 46116 *Irish Guardsman*, bound for Crewe. (D.K.Jones coll.)

10.   Known as The Dana, the public footbridge has provided a link between the town and the prison. The subway has served most passengers, but there was an independent footbridge at the far end of the platforms until 1961. "Sprinter" no. 150141 is working the 17.15 to Crewe on 9th May 1989. (P.G.Barnes)

11.   The 13.24 to Cardiff is approaching on 8th August 1990 and it is worked by DMU no. 155312. Royal Mail traffic is evident, as is the bridge containing the mailbag conveyor system. (V.Mitchell)

12.   The retired goods shed was adapted to serve the engineers, who had adopted the yard. We view Crewe Junction from a Marylebone to Wrexham train on 26th June 2008. The Shrewsbury & Chester Railway's first station was sited on the left and was in use until 1st June 1849 when "United" came into use. It was for long known as "General", in GWR days and beyond. (V.Mitchell)

13.   We look north along platform 4 and see DMU no. 158823 at No. 3. This platform had become little used, but the operation of the London-Wrexham service between 2008 and 2011 increased its usage, as there were five trains each way on weekdays, plus three on Sundays. Crewe Junction Box is in the distance. The date is 9th January 2008. (R.Geach)

14.   All platforms were accessible via the subway, except No. 3, which had steps from the south end of the entrance canopy. No. 3 can take 13 coaches, Nos 5 and 6 take five and Nos 4 and 7 take 15. Often two short trains occupy one long platform. (V.Mitchell)

15.　　Platform 7 was serving the "Cathedrals Explorer" 12-coach tour of England and Wales from London on 11th May 2013. Bays 4 and 5 were commonly used by stopping trains to Birmingham as well as the Heart of Wales Line; they were used for other local services, as well. The connection to the Hereford line from platform 3 (right) had been restored in April 2010 and the semaphore signal erected, a rare event in the 21st century. (V.Mitchell)

16.　　Minutes later, the train departed for Porthmadog, hauled by no. 97304 *John Tiley* and no. 97303, both in the bright yellow livery of Network Rail. Included is part of Severn Bridge Junction Box, which was an LNWR creation, with 180 levers. The journey included Caernarvon, Carlisle and Whitby. (V.Mitchell)

17.   Passing Crewe Bank Box on 5th April 1988 is no. 37894 with the 08.05 Abercwmboi to Ellesmere Port coal train. The 45-lever box was built in 1943 and was in regular use until 2nd February 2007. The up goods loop on the left was still in use, as was the down siding, which served a coal concentration depot. This had earlier been an oil depot, tanks are still visible and are shown on map II. Also evident on it are sidings for a saw mill and for a maltings. (P.D.Shannon)

The Sentinel
Volume 1
1875-1930

EVER WATCHFUL & ON THE ALERT

TRADE MARK

W. J. Hughes
and
Joseph L. Thomas

DAVID &
CHARLES

Alley & MacLellan of Glasgow started to build the famous 'Sentinel' steam waggons in 1905, but long before that their trade name, 'Sentinel', had been carried world-wide on many other products, including stationary and marine steam engines,

Later the Sentinel Waggon Works, known affectionately as 'The Sentinel', became a separate entity, and through the famous 'Super' and 'D.G.' waggons developed the design until with the 'S'-type it became known as the Rolls-Royce of steam waggons.

Other products included steam tractors and portable engines, the well-known Sentinel-Cammell railcars, and rail locomotives for both freight and passenger traffic.

← 18. Top right on map II is the Sentinel Wagon Works and facing is the cover and summary of part of its 1973 history. (There was always a double "g" in their spelling of wagon.) Most of their boilers were unusual in being vertical, with an inner and outer barrel. The water was between them and inside the tubes, which spanned the inner one. This part could be lowered into a pit for easy maintenance. Most locomotives were supplied to industrial users, but the Wisbech & Upwell Tramway had a fleet (see *Branch Line to Upwell*) and by 1931, there were 55 on the LNER. (One of the former gained fame as the fictional *Toby the Tram Engine*). The railcars (lower) were introduced in 1922 and were sent world wide. A set was recovered from Egypt and can be seen in picture 17 in our *Aylesbury to Rickmansworth* album, undergoing restoration at the Buckinghamshire Railway Centre. (D&C)

19. Locomotives were not built between 1937 and 1945. A fleet of 88 six-wheeled tipper lorries went to the Argentine Coal Board in 1950. It was the final batch of road vehicles from the works. Rolls Royce later took over and steam engine production ceased in 1958. However, 37 survive on private railways. This is one of a batch of 12 built for the Dorman Long Steelworks in Middlesbrough in 1956. It has an oil-fired vertical boiler, behind the cab, and is seen on 16th August 1955. (B.Connell/H.Davies)

HADNALL

IV. The 1901 survey includes a weighing machine marked W.M. There was a population of 564 at that time. The cottages on the right were for railway employees.

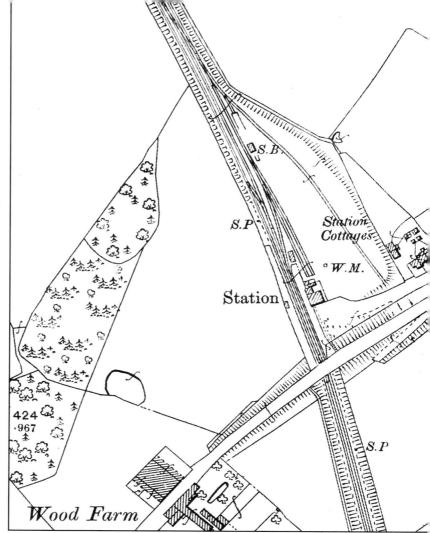

20. An early postcard includes a horse-box in the siding behind the down platform and a horse and cart at the other end of that platform. Intricate chimney pots were intended to impress the passengers.
(P.Laming coll.)

21.	A late 1930s postcard features a southbound express and timber in the platform to minimise damage to milk churn rims. Near the rear of the train is the signal box, which was in use until 9th November 1965. (P.Laming coll.)

22.	This was a favourite reversal point for locomotives on test runs from Crewe Works. We can be impressed by the exotic gardens on 20th September 1958. On the left is an early container. (R.M.Casserley)

23.   The signs and lamps have gone and so this view must have been recorded soon after the station closed to passengers on 2nd May 1960. Sadly no details were recorded. The train will soon pass the sidings for an Army Ordnance Depot, which was used in both wars. (P. Ward/SLS)

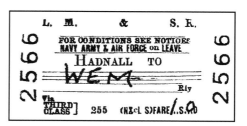

24.   Goods traffic ceased here on 2nd November 1964 and the empty yard is seen in 1967, along with the parcels shed (right). At the far end of the canopy projects the ventilator over the toilet for gentlemen. (Stations UK)

25.   The two locomotives described in caption 16 are seen more fully on 28th May 2011. They are heading the "Statesman Rail Charter" to Aberystwyth, by which time the buildings had become a desirable residence. To the south, there was still a signal box at Harlescott Crossing. It was built in 1882 and had 28 levers, but use of the word "Crossing" was discontinued in later years. (J.Whitehouse)

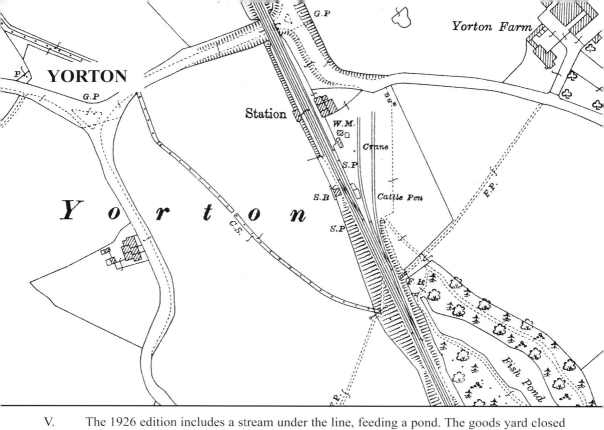

V.   The 1926 edition includes a stream under the line, feeding a pond. The goods yard closed on 6th April 1964, the crane shown being rated at 5 tons.

26.   This is a northward view in 1955. Passengers had to use the crossing in the foreground. The spelling was initially "Yarnton". North of the station was Tilley Crossing; it closed on 17th January 1971. (Stations UK)

27.   This closer view is from 20th September 1958 and includes a traditional sack barrow. Behind the camera is the 1882 signal box, which had 18 levers. It closed on 15th April 1973 and was moved to Arley on the Severn Valley Railway in 1976. (R.M.Casserley)

28.   Running in on 24th April 2013 is no. 175013. Passengers had to shelter on the right, as the building had become a private house. Platform 1 was suitable for two coaches, while No. 2 could take three. (P.D.Shannon)

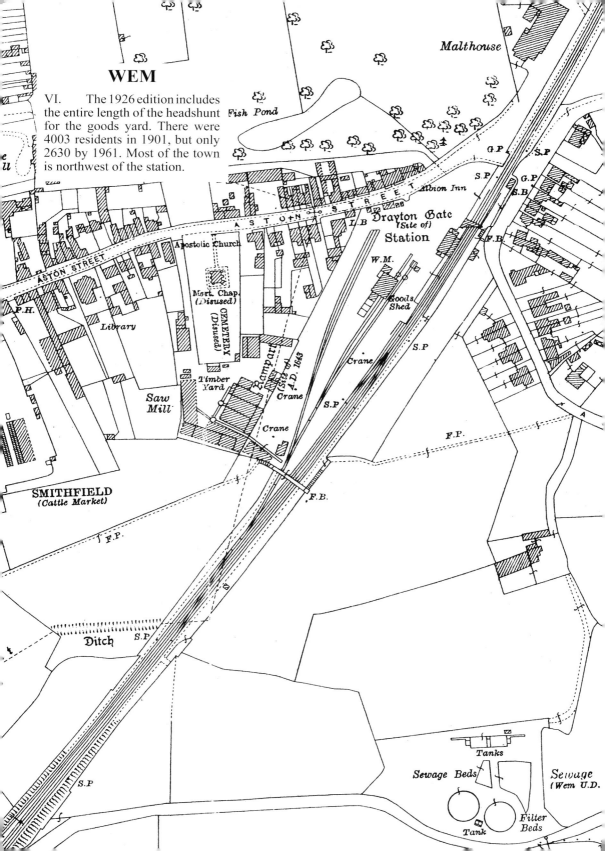

WEM

VI. The 1926 edition includes the entire length of the headshunt for the goods yard. There were 4003 residents in 1901, but only 2630 by 1961. Most of the town is northwest of the station.

Malthouse

Fish Pond

ASTON STREET

Albion Inn

Drayton Gate
(Site of)
Station

G.P.
S.P.
S.P.
G.P.
S.B.
F.B.

Apostolic Church

ASTON STREET

I.B

W.M.

Goods
Shed

P.H.

Library

Mort. Chap.
(Disused)

CEMETERY
(Disused)

Rampart

(Site of
A.D. 1643)

Timber
Yard

S.P.

Crane

Saw
Mill

Crane

Crane

Crane

S.P.

F.P.

A

SMITHFIELD
(Cattle Market)

F.B.

F.P.

Ditch

S.P.

S.P.

Tanks

Sewage Beds

Sewage
(Wem U.D.

Filter
Beds

Tank

29.   A 1954 panorama features the up waiting room and its wide brick-built fireplace backing. Great care was taken in such wooden buildings and much labour was required in winter time. (Stations UK)

30.   The footbridge was provided in 1923. The economical form of roofing at least kept the snow off the steps. A BR class 4MT 4-6-0 is northbound. (P. Ward/SLS coll.)

31.	The crane can be seen; it was rated at five tons. The goods yard was in use until 5th April 1971. The public footbridge can be found in the middle of the map. (R.M.Casserley coll.)

32.	"Hall" class 4-6-0 no. 6998 *Burton Agnes Hall* of 1949 departs with a stopping train in 1959. It is now resident at the Didcot Railway Centre. Wem North signal box functioned in 1942 to 1948 and served military sidings. It was later moved to Nantwich station. (D.K.Jones)

33.	No. 47159 passes through with the 11.40 Paignton to Manchester on 6th September 1975. The 1883 box had 35 levers and a gate wheel, the latter being visible. Train operating numbers would soon not be shown, as fewer signalling staff had sight of trains. (T.Heavyside)

34.	Running through on 7th April 1984 is no. 40044 with a Manchester to Swansea "Footex". The twin starting signals were needed, as the footbridge could cause visual obstruction. (J.Whitehouse)

35.   No. 37884 roars through on 17th June 1989, hauling steel coils from Ravenscraig to tinplate works at Trostre and Ebbw Vale. Loaded steel wagons would also run in the other direction, from South Wales to Shotton. The white levers are the ones out of use. (P.D.Shannon)

36.   A train with a short formation runs into a station with a short name while long welded rails flank a long queue of passengers. Seen on 20th April 2013 is no. 153312, bound for Shrewsbury. Note the revised signalling, when compared with picture 34. (P.D.Shannon)

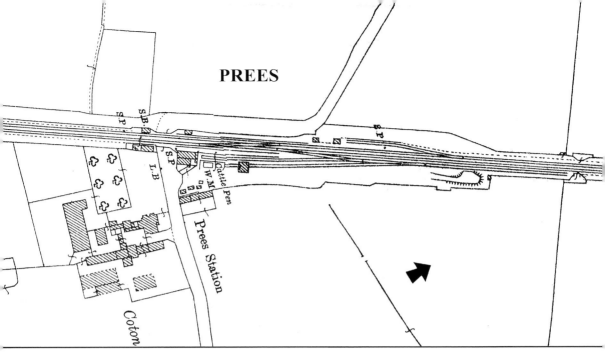

PREES

VII.   Here is another station set in thinly populated countryside, with only railway cottages showing on the 1926 edition. The population of the village was 1892 in 1901 and 2128 in 1961. Its centre is more than a mile to the east.

37.   Two low roofed six-wheeled coaches spoil the profile of this express during the transition to bogie coaches around the turn of the century. The locomotive is a "19 inch Goods" LNWR 4-6-0; the measurement refers to the cylinder diameter. (Bentley coll.)

38.   A well worn path between the wicket gates is evident. They had been locked by the signalman prior to the departure south of class 6F 2-6-0 no. 42955. This 1950s view is from the signal box. (W.A.Camwell/SLS)

39.   From the same vantage point, we can see the extent of the goods yard and the size of its shed. Traffic was extensive in 1954, but it ceased on 6th October 1964. (Stations UK)

40.   A new DMU departs north in the mid-1950s, when the "Cat's whiskers" were still in fashion. The LMS "Hawkseye" boards were always set at 45° to the platform edge. (W.A.Camwell/SLS)

41.   More steel passes along the route, this time in 1957 behind Ivatt class 2MT 2-6-0 no. 46415. The first of this design appeared in 1946 and 128 were built subsequently. The goods shed doors are open and therein was a 30cwt crane. (Stations UK)

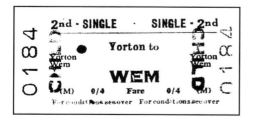

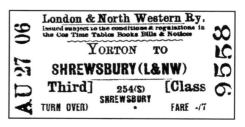

42.   Clearer signs were provided by BR and devoid of a nickname. The 17.23 Crewe to Shrewsbury was recorded on 6th September 1975, when passengers could still enjoy splendid views from both ends of the train. (T.Heavyside)

43.   Recorded on the same day was no. 47267 with the 11.10 Penzance to Manchester. Staffing of the station had ceased on 19th June 1966. (T.Heavyside)

44.   We complete our study that day with an examination of platform height. This is probably the original and there is no evidence of the portable steps widely seen on former GWR stations. (T.Heavyside)

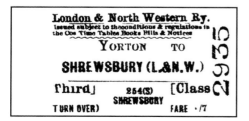

London & North Western Ry.

Issued subject to the conditions & regulations in the Coy Time Tables Books Bills & Notices

YORTON   TO

SHREWSBURY (L.&N.W.)

Third]   254(S)   [Class
              SHREWSBURY
TURN OVER)   FARE ·/7

2935

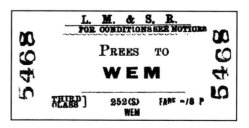

L. M. & S. R.

FOR CONDITIONS SEE NOTICES

PREES   TO

WEM

THIRD]   252(S)   FARE -/8 P
CLASS   WEM

5468   5468

45.   The 25-lever frame dates from the completion of the box in 1881 and it is seen in May 1989. The traditional rag is centre stage, it being required to prevent damp hands from tarnishing the bright steel of the levers. (P.G.Barnes)

46.   Modern windows had been fitted and barriers installed by the time that no. 175002 had been recorded heading north on 8th June 2013. The box should have vanished by that time, but resignalling of the route had been delayed. (P.D.Shannon)

SOUTH OF WHITCHURCH

47.   Whitchurch Cambrian Junction box was immediately south of the station and the former Cambrian Railway to Ellesmere can be seen curving away from the Shrewsbury line on the right. The date is 12th May 1967. (R.J.Essery/R.S.Carpenter)

48.   We move to the left to see the junction fully and the bridge over Station Road. The ex-GWR branch had closed on 16th January 1965, but the 45-lever box remained in use until 8th June 1969. (P.J.Garland/R.S.Carpenter)

WHITCHURCH (SHROPSHIRE)

49.   Running near the goods yard in about 1925 is no. 5036 *Novelty*, of the LNWR "Precedent" class. Further north, it will reach Whitchurch Chester Junction, where there was a 45-lever signal box until 15th June 1969. (G.Coltas Trust)

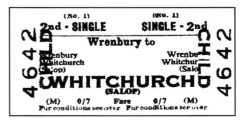

VIII.   The 1926 edition has the location of pictures 47 and 48 on the left of this map. The upper line on the right is to Malpas and Tattenhall, while the lower one is our route to Crewe. The streets at the top converge near the town centre. Note that there are private sidings for wood and iron.

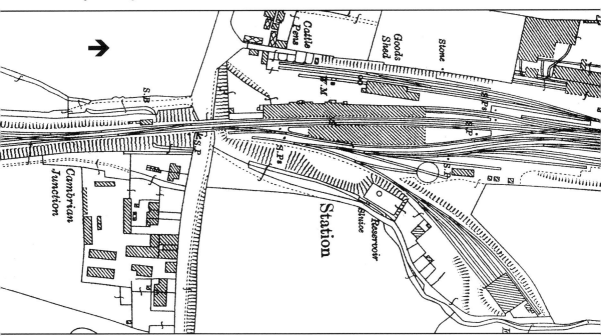

50.   Creeping in from the south is Stanier class 5MT 2-6-0 no. 42983 on 19th May 1951. Almost 250 of these locomotives were built from 1926 onwards. The line on the left leads to the engine shed, albeit indirectly. (Bentley coll.)

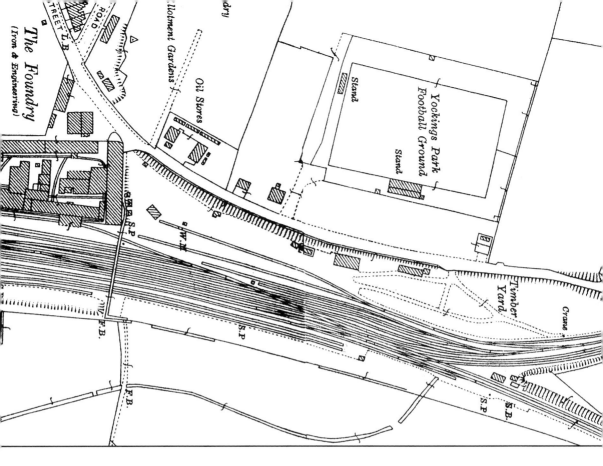

The following labels appear on the map:

The Foundry (Iron & Engineering)

STREET T.B.
ROAD

Allotment Gardens

Oil Stores

dry

Yockings Park Football Ground

Stand

Stand

Timber Yard

Crane

S.P.

W.B.

F.B.

S.P.

F.B.

S.P.

S.P.

S.B.

51.   This is the north end of the station in August 1953, with the well sheltered bay platform on the right. This was often used by trains for Chester, via Malpas. (H.C.Casserley)

WHITCHURCH

52.   The island platform becomes apparent in this photograph from about 1962. The turntable is to the right of the water tank. (Stations UK)

53.	This southward view from 18th May 1963 reveals that the footbridge had lost its roof, but that the platforms had been re-roofed. Compare with picture 51. We are looking at the rear of a southbound train. (P.Kingston)

54.	The frontage was photographed on 12th January 1967, with two Fords in the lead. On the left is the goods shed, with a BR delivery van adjacent. (R.J.Essery/R.S.Carpenter)

55.   The signal box hides the goods yard, which closed on 1st October 1976. The 14.14 Crewe to Shrewsbury is approaching the station on 6th September 1975 and is seen from the bridge in the background of picture 57. The water tank was still standing; it is seen above the train. (T.Heavyside)

56.   The 09.30 Shrewsbury to Crewe was recorded arriving on 16th August 1984. Most of the buildings had been destroyed and basic bus shelters were provided for passengers. The suffix "Salop" was applied for some years, but was changed to "Shropshire" on 9th December 2007. (D.H.Mitchell)

Other views of this station can be found in our *Oswestry to Whitchurch* album.

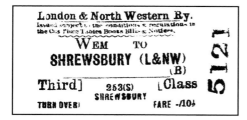

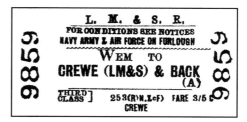

57.	The 09.15 Liverpool to Cardiff arrives behind no. 37408 on 24th June 1989. For long known as Whitchurch Goods Yard, the 1897 box had 55 levers and was boarded up in 2007. The signals were disconnected on 19th April 2011 and the box was demolished on 5th August 2012. (T.Heavyside)

58.	Ex-LMS "Jubilee" class no. 45596 *Bahamas* stands at Whitchurch on 26th March 1994. It was at the head of "The Welsh Marches Express", a steam special operating between Crewe and Worcester Shrub Hill via Shrewsbury and Hereford. (M.P.Turvey)

EAST OF WHITCHURCH

59. Pictured outside the shed on 6th December 1953 are nos. 42566, 42263 (2-6-4Ts) and, on the right, ex-GWR 4-6-0 no. 7820 *Dinmore Manor*. This subsequently retired to the West Somerset Railway. (F.A.Wycherley coll.)

60. This is a panorama from the end of the footbridge on 8th August 1964. Underground cables would soon eliminate the need for the multitude of porcelain insulators. (Bentley coll.)

61. Over the pit on 30th June 1956 is 2-6-4T no. 42321 and inside is sister no. 41167. The rural setting is apparent in this and the view below. (H.C.Casserley)

WRENBURY

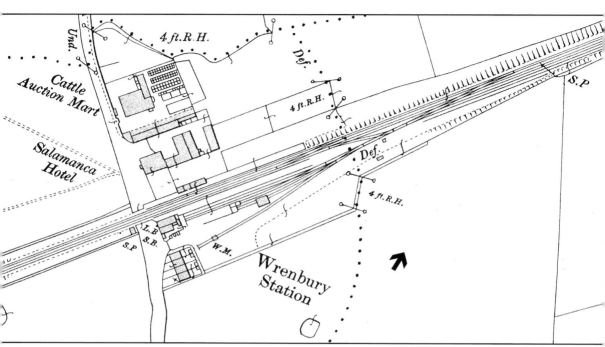

IX.   The establishment of a cattle market close to a station brought much extra railway traffic, some of it over long distances. This is its setting in 1910.

62.   This postcard view is from the southwest and has the station building centre, with the railway staff cottages on the right. The village housed 491 in 1901 and 815 in 1961. (P.Laming coll.)

63.   A more personal card includes a demonstration of how to move a loaded milk churn without lifting it. More churns adorn the other platform, beyond which is the goods shed and a horse box. (P.Laming coll.)

64.   We now have four pictures from 1967. Here we see the back of the staff cottages and the house for the station master. The station had become unstaffed on 19th September 1966, hence the neglected flower beds. (Stations UK)

65.   A view in the other direction includes the small goods shed and many point rods. There had earlier been private sidings for Pooles and Trufood Ltd. (Stations UK)

66.   The yard had a two-ton crane, but traffic ceased on 6th July 1964. The points had gone, but the crossover remained. (R.J.Essery/R.S.Carpenter)

67. The southwest elevation in good lighting conditions can be enjoyed. The complexities of the old chimneys and the new lighting are unusual. The Mini was likewise when introduced by Morris in 1959. (R.J.Essery/R.S.Carpenter)

68. The 1882 signal box had a 20-lever frame, which was still in use on 15th September 2013, when no. 66415 was photographed with imported coal. It was loaded at Portbury, near Bristol, and was destined for Rugeley Power Station via Basford Hall Yard, where there was a crew change. (P.D.Shannon)

SOUTH OF NANTWICH

69. Market Drayton Junction was ½ mile southwest of the station and the route from Wellington joined here. The signal box ceased to function following a fire on 16th January 1967. The former GWR line closed that year, although passenger services had ceased in 1963. (Milepost 92½)

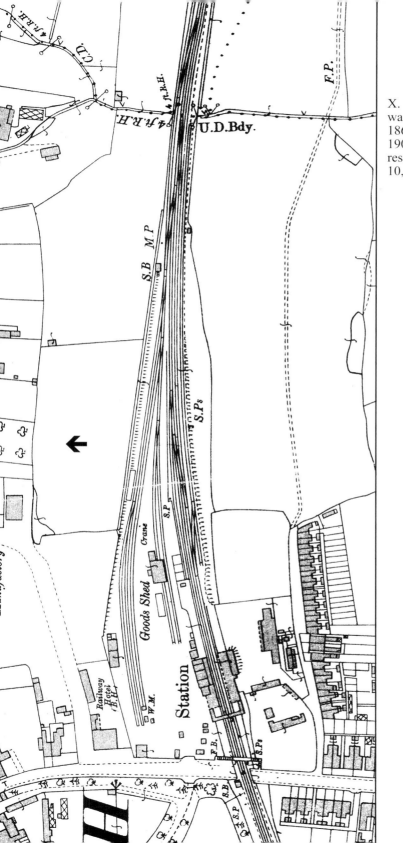

NANTWICH

X.   The suffix "Junction" was used by Bradshaw in 1864-1916, but it is not on this 1909 map. There were 7772 residents in 1901, this rising to 10,880 in 1961.

70.   This 1949 view from the level crossing is much clearer than one from the footbridge. The running-in board offers a wide choice of destinations for the ill informed. The town had been noted for salt, but production ceased at around the time that the railway arrived. (Stations UK)

71.   A glimpse from one of the small open ventilators on the bridge on 28th June 1956 reveals 4300 class 2-6-0 no. 4316, with freight from Oxley to Crewe via Wellington. The complexity of cranks and pulleys is evident. (H.F.Wheeller/R.S.Carpenter)

↓ 72. It is 30th September 1952 and blowing off is no. 45553 *Canada*, a "Jubilee" class 4-6-0. On the left is the lamp room, a busy place with so many signals in the district. (Bentley coll.)

73.   Three photographs from 5th August 1963 provide a comprehensive survey of the premises. Here we have some fine canopy brackets near 2-6-2T class 2P no. 41204, as it runs in with the 12.15 from Wellington. (R.M.Casserley)

74.   The iron rails mounted in the road mark the boundary of the weigh bridge; its office and instruments are on the left. In the background is the goods yard, which closed on 4th September 1972. It had a 5-ton crane. (R.M.Casserley)

↓ 75.   The rods between the tracks had been added prior to the closure of Goods Yard Box on 3rd December 1949. The small buildings on the right were used mainly for parcels traffic. (R.M.Casserley)

76.   Known originally as Station Box, it had been built in 1948 and fitted with a 30-lever frame. It had earlier been in use at Wem and is seen in 1966. (Stations UK)

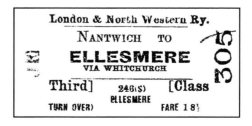

Extract from Bradshaw's Guide 1866,
reprinted by Middleton Press.

NANTWICH.

POPULATION, 6,225.

Telegraph station at Crewe, 4¼ miles.

HOTEL.—Lamb.

Here is a cruciform church, with pinnacled tower. Lord Byron, who occupied *Dorford Hall*, 1643, was defeated by Fairfax. This place was formerly celebrated for its salt mines, but is now famous for its cheese.

WRENBURY Station.

The *Nantwich and Market Drayton* line runs out here, passing through the stations of AUDLEM and ADDERLEY to

MARKET DRAYTON, the trade of which does not appear to be in a very flourishing condition, but which, no doubt, will receive an impetus after the completion of the railway through to Wellington, which is rapidly progressing.

77.   The 16.02 Crewe to Cardiff was recorded on 4th April 1980, with no. 25220 in charge. The box name still carried the word STATION. (T.Heavyside)

78. DMU no. M50721 is leading, while working the 17.23 Crewe to Shrewsbury on 1st June 1981. Simple shelters were provided, as the building had other uses by that time. Both platforms could take five coaches. (T.Heavyside)

79. No. 66174 approaches the station on 26th May 2013, with an engineers train. It was the 10.00 from Craven Arms to Basford Hall. (P.D.Shannon)

EAST OF NANTWICH

80.   The name Newcastle Crossing was applied to a station here from 2nd January 1911 to 1st April 1918. The road became the A52 in 1919, when numbering was introduced. The locomotive is class 5 4-6-0 no. 44681 and is seen on 4th July 1953. The box had 15 levers and closed on 16th April 1967, when automatic barriers arrived. (Bentley coll.)

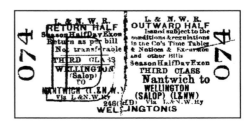

WILLASTON

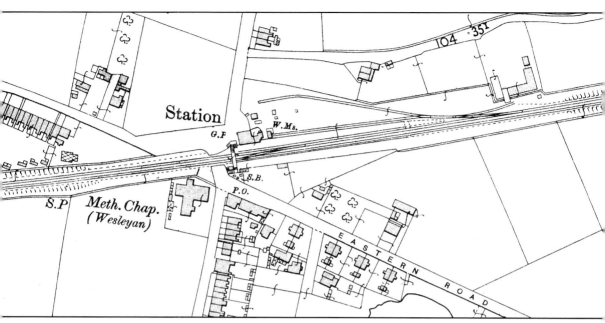

XI.   This is the last village before reaching Crewe, unlike which it did not grow. The census in 1901 showed 2400 souls and in 2001 listed 2277. The 1911 map shows no crane in the goods yard.

81.   A train arrives from the west on 28th September 1952 and the signalman is profiled as he waits with his hand on the gate wheel. Passenger service here was withdrawn on 6th December 1954. (Bentley coll.)

87.   We now have two views from 1st November 1958. The new signal box would come into use on 10th December following. Its 20-lever frame was in use until 28th October 1984. (Bentley coll.)

88.   Seldom are sequential signal boxes pictured, but here we have classic LNWR and BR examples. However, the flat roofed design was evolved during World War II, as concrete gave good protection during air raids. (Bentley coll.)

89.   No. D1023 *Western Fusilier* was heading the "Western Memorial" tour on 29th January 1977. It had started at Paddington and used the "North & Western" route to Crewe. It continued to Chester and returned to London. (J.Whitehouse)

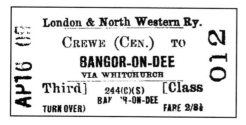

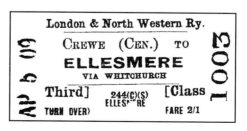

90.   Gresty Lane shed was built in 1870 jointly by the GWR and LNWR. It was enlarged by doubling its length in 1913. Nearest on 29th May 1960 is BR class 2P 2-6-2T no. 41231. (R.S.Carpenter)

91.   A close-up of classmate no. 41241 is from 30th September 1962. Production of this class was begun by the LMS in 1946. The shed closed on 6th July 1963. (M.J.Stretton)

92.   Moving nearer to Crewe, we have three views which include both Gresty Lane signal boxes. This is No. 1, which is shown on the next map, near its centre. On the left is the Permanent Way Works, while centre is an express for the West of England headed by no. 249, a Bowen-Cooke "Prince of Wales" class 3P. (Bentley coll.)

93.   Gresty Lane No. 1 is seen again, but on 25th March 1961. The overhead electrification had recently been completed in the Crewe area. The box had opened in January 1899, but its original frame had been replaced by a longer miniature lever frame. This was superseded by a panel in 1978 and it was still in use in 2013. (Bentley coll.)

94.   *Western Fusilier* is seen again on 29th January 1977. The C-C class 52 was built in 1963 and became one of the National Railway Museum's treasures. No. 2 Box had 18 levers and closed on 28th October 1984. The electrification went no further west. (T.Heavyside)

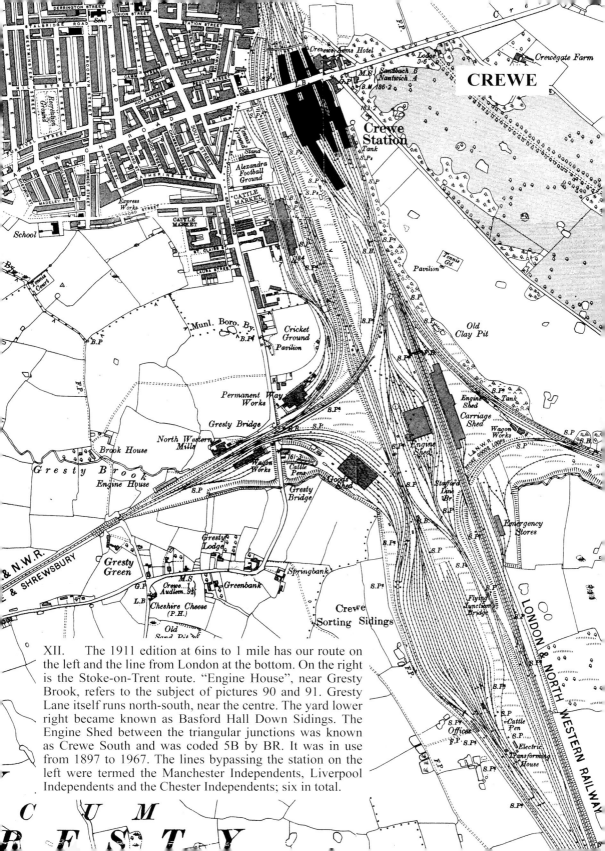

CREWE

XII.   The 1911 edition at 6ins to 1 mile has our route on the left and the line from London at the bottom. On the right is the Stoke-on-Trent route. "Engine House", near Gresty Brook, refers to the subject of pictures 90 and 91. Gresty Lane itself runs north-south, near the centre. The yard lower right became known as Basford Hall Down Sidings. The Engine Shed between the triangular junctions was known as Crewe South and was coded 5B by BR. It was in use from 1897 to 1967. The lines bypassing the station on the left were termed the Manchester Independents, Liverpool Independents and the Chester Independents; six in total.

95.　　Initially there were only two tracks, but two through ones were soon added. Major expansions took place in 1867 and again in 1887. More through lines arrived and a third island platform came between 1903 to 1906. This card was posted in 1917. (P.Laming coll.)

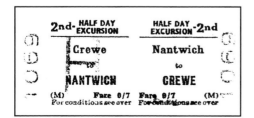

96.   A Shrewsbury express leaves in about 1929, with the roof board showing Aberystwyth on the leading coach. Heading it is ex-LNWR "Precedent" class LMS no. 5042 *The Auditor*. (R.S.Carpenter coll.)

97.   The roofing eventually covered an amazing 12 acres, but it became a hazard during the bombing of World War II. This postcard is probably from around 1930, as female legs are visible. (P.Laming coll.)

98.　　Platform 4 was recorded in 1948, before the renumbering. The 1940 flat-roofed South Junction signal box is out of view. It had 227 miniature levers and closed on 21st July 1985. Its predecessor of 1907 had 274 such levers. (Stations UK)

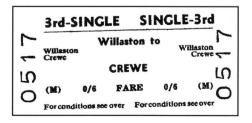

3rd-SINGLE　　SINGLE-3rd

Willaston to

Willaston
Crewe

Willaston
Crewe

CREWE

(M)　　0/6　　FARE　　0/6　　(M)

For conditions see over　　For conditions see over

0517

0517

London & North Western Ry

Issued subject to the conditions & regulations in the Cos Time Tables Books Bills & Notices

TATTENHALL　　TO

CREWE(L.&N.W.)

VIA WAVERTON

Third]　251(S.)(vW)　[Class

CREWE　　FARE 1/6½

2 AU 16

076

99.   The south end of the station was photographed from a moving train, with smoke spoiling the view as so often happened. The year is 1948. (Stations UK)

100.   This panorama is from about 1955 and includes platform 2 and 'B' Box. The latter remained in use until 10th April 1960. (Stations UK)

101.   Working vans on 16th June 1957 is ex-LNWR 2-4-2T no. 46680, while tanks are being hauled by ex-LMS "Jubilee" class 4-6-0 no. 45623 *Palestine*. (Bentley coll.)

102.   Pictured on 19th September 1959 is ex-GWR 2-6-2T no. 4158, with the 12.52pm departure for Wellington. This and the next view feature the south end bays. (H.C.Casserley)

↓ 103. Also on a Wellington service is ex-GWR 4-6-0 no. 7802 *Bradley Manor* on 19th April 1962. It was built in 1938 and withdrawn in 1965, only to be rescued for a retirement on the Severn Valley Railway. (B.W.L.Brooksbank)

104.   Reversing empty stock on 16th June 1984 is no. 33032. Class 33s spent most of their working lives on the Southern Region, but a few had their final years on trips to Cardiff. (T.Heavyside)

105.   The same locomotive was recorded in the opposite direction. A major £14.3m remodelling and resignalling of the station area took place in 1984 to 1985 to thoroughly streamline and modernise the outdated 'steam age' track layout to suit modern traffic. For example, the number of points and crossings was reduced from 285 to 110, and it proved possible to close most of the west side island, save for one through platform, concentrating traffic on the centre and east islands; non-stop trains, previously restricted to 20-30mph could now pass at 80mph on the realigned fast lines through the centre of the station. The new Crewe Signalling Centre opened on 21st July 1985, replacing the obsolete Crewe North Junction and South Junction wartime boxes. (T.Heavyside)

106.   'A' Box lasted until 1985 and was moved to become an exhibit at the Crewe Heritage Centre, north of the station. It was built in 1906 and had a 26 miniature lever power frame. (E.Wilmshurst)

Many other views of this station and also Crewe Works can be found in our *Stafford to Chester* album.

107.   We are looking south from platform 5 on 11th October 1994, as no. 153373 departs for Shrewsbury. It will curve to the right beyond the lines of locomotives standing in Crewe Diesel Depot. (A.C.Hartless)

108.   Two photographs from 25th February 1995 can now be enjoyed. Bay platforms 7 and 8 occupy the space between the south ends of numbers 6 and 11. No. 310091 is in Network SouthEast livery, as it waits to work the 11.48 to Rugby. These bays were used mostly by stopping services to Shrewsbury. Barrows fill the space between 8 and 11. (A.C.Hartless)

109.   A quiet period at platform 6 enables us to study the architecture and witness no. 43080 with the 06.50 Edinburgh to Reading at platform 5. This could take 13 coaches. No. 12 was the longest, it could accommodate 22. (A.C.Hartless)

110. Tidy environs surround no. 153308 as it waits to run all stations to Shrewsbury on 11th November 1999. These cars were listed as Super Sprinters and were produced by Hunslet-Barclay, with Cummins engines. Bays 3 and 4 are in the left background. (P.Jones)

111. We finish our survey with two pictures from 7th September 2009. Speeding through is a Pendolino, probably running from Glasgow to Euston. On the right is a class 323 entering platforms 1 and 2, from Manchester Piccadilly. (V.Mitchell)

112. Standing at platform 5 is a London Midland class 350 working from Liverpool to Birmingham New Street. Platform 6 was empty for a brief period. The 1985 Crewe Signalling Centre was erected on the site of the Crewe North engine shed. (V.Mitchell)

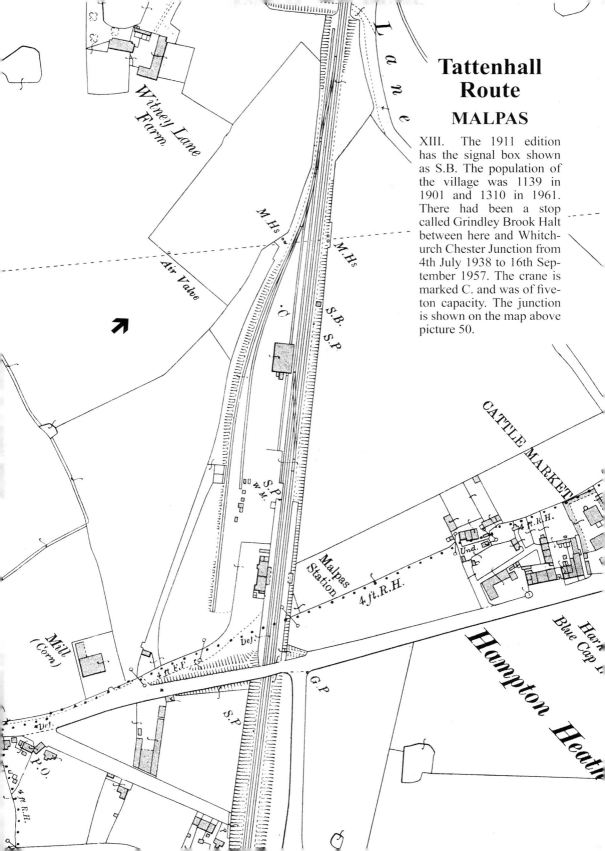

Tattenhall Route

MALPAS

XIII. The 1911 edition has the signal box shown as S.B. The population of the village was 1139 in 1901 and 1310 in 1961. There had been a stop called Grindley Brook Halt between here and Whitchurch Chester Junction from 4th July 1938 to 16th September 1957. The crane is marked C. and was of five-ton capacity. The junction is shown on the map above picture 50.

Witney Lane Farm

M.Hs

M.Hs

Air Valve

S.B.
S.P

C.

S.P
W.M.

CATTLE MARKET

Und.

4 ft. R.H.

Malpas Station

4 ft. R.H.

Horn
Blue Cap I.

Mill (Corn)

Del.

Del.

P.O.

4 ft R.H.

S.P.

G.P

Hampton Heath

113.   To the right of the locomotive is the small signal box, which was open until 16th December 1963. The route was double track throughout. (P.Laming coll.)

114.   Cattle wagons are in the goods yard, as a horse walks away from the station, possibly adding to the debris on the road. This would definitely increase on market day. (P.Laming coll.)

115.   Passengers could use the crossing in the foreground, although the map shows one path down from the road. On the right is the large parcels shed; the many milk churns evident would not dwell long enough to use it. (LOSA)

896	L. M. & S. R. FOR CONDITIONS SEE NOTICES NAVY ARMY & AIR FORCE on LEAVE MALPAS TO **CHESTER (LMS)** THIRD CLASS] 249NXcL(S) FARE 1/6 C CHESTER	896

0020	3rd-SINGLE SINGLE-3rd **Malpas** to Malpas Malpas Waverton Waverton **WAVERTON** (M) 1/8 FARE 1/8 (M) For conditions see over For conditions see over	0020

3817	L M. & S R FOR CONDITIONS SEE NOTICES MALPAS TO **WHITCHURCH (L.M.&S.)** THIRD] 24c FARE 1/0½ C CLASS WHITE LMS	3817

0126	CHILD	3rd-SINGLE Malpas to **BROXTON or** **GRINDLEY BROOK** FARE 9/4	CHILD	0126
		For conditions see over		

116.   A panorama from the bridge in 1949 includes part of the goods yard, which was in use until 4th November 1963. A chimney from a single storey outbuilding usually served the boiler for washing clothes. (Stations UK)

117.   Passenger traffic ceased on 16th September 1957. The well kept gardens are seen from a passing train on 27th August 1954, as arriving parcels are carried across the line. (R.M.Casserley)

BROXTON

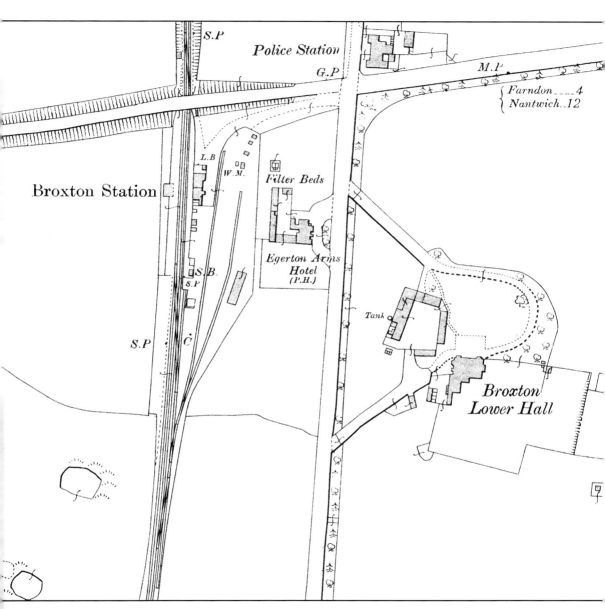

S.P

Police Station

G.P

M.P

Farndon ____4
Nantwich..12

L.B

W..M.

Filter Beds

Broxton Station

S.B.

S.P

Egerton Arms
Hotel
(P.H.)

Tank

S.P   C.

Broxton
Lower Hall

XIV.   The 1911 edition includes a country mansion, an inn and a police station, all with nearby buildings to house equine power for road transport. Goods and passenger closure dates are as for Malpas.

118.   The signal box closed on 16th December 1963 and the line closed completely in the following year. We witness ex-Midland Railway class 2P 4-4-0 no. 40413 about to depart with the 2.14pm Chester to Whitchurch service, on 1st October 1955. (W.A.Camwell/SLS)

119.   A view after closure to passengers includes a parcels shed, plus one raised on staddle stones. These prevented vermin entering buildings used for storage of animal feedstuff and seeds. (Stations UK)

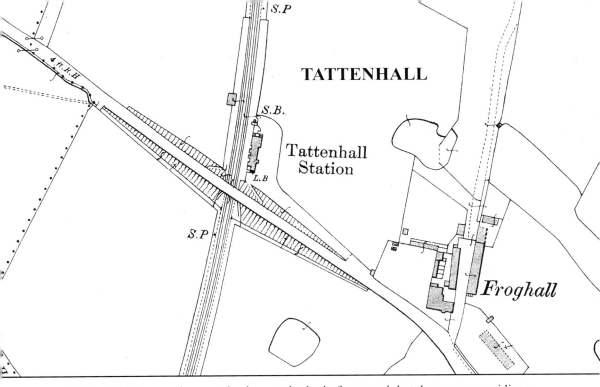

XV. The 1911 map shows paths down to both platforms and that there were no sidings.

120.　　Tattenhall Road station served passengers until 16th September 1966 and was on the Crewe-Chester main line. It can be seen in pictures 94-96 in *Stafford to Chester*. The station shown was closer to the village, which housed 975 in 1901. The closure dates were as for the previous two stations. (Stations UK)

MP Middleton Press
EVOLVING THE ULTIMATE RAIL ENCYCLOPEDIA

Easebourne Lane, Midhurst, West Sussex.
GU29 9AZ   Tel:01730 813169
www.middletonpress.co.uk   email:info@middletonpress.co.uk
A-978 0 906520 B- 978 1 873793 C- 978 1 901706 D-978 1 904474
E - 978 1 906008   F - 978 1 908174

All titles listed below were in print at time of publication - please check current availability by looking at our
website - *www.middletonpress.co.uk* or by requesting a Brochure which includes our
LATEST RAILWAY TITLES also our TRAMWAY, TROLLEYBUS, MILITARY and COASTAL series

A

Abergavenny to Merthyr C 91 8
Abertillery & Ebbw Vale Lines D 84 5
Aberystwyth to Carmarthen E 90 1
Allhallows - Branch Line to A 62 8
Alton - Branch Lines to A 11 6
Andover to Southampton A 82 6
Ascot - Branch Lines around A 64 2
Ashburton - Branch Line to B 95 4
Ashford - Steam to Eurostar B 67 1
Ashford to Dover A 48 2
Austrian Narrow Gauge D 04 3
Avonmouth - BL around D 42 5
Aylesbury to Rugby D 91 3

B

Baker Street to Uxbridge D 90 6
Bala to Llandudno E 87 1
Banbury to Birmingham D 27 2
Banbury to Cheltenham E 63 5
Bangor to Holyhead F 01 7
Bangor to Portmadoc E 72 7
Barking to Southend C 80 2
Barmouth to Pwllheli E 53 6
Barry - Branch Lines around D 50 0
Bartlow - Branch Lines to F 27 7
Bath Green Park to Bristol C 36 9
Bath to Evercreech Junction A 60 4
Beamish 40 years on rails E94 9
Bedford to Wellingborough D 31 9
Birmingham to Wolverhampton E253
Bletchley to Cambridge D 94 4
Bletchley to Rugby E 07 9
Bodmin - Branch Lines around B 83 1
Bournemouth to Evercreech Jn A 46 8
Bournemouth to Weymouth A 57 4
Bradshaw's Guide 1866 F 05 5
Bradshaw's History F18 5
Bradshaw's Rail Times 1850 F 13 0
Bradshaw's Rail Times 1895 F 11 6
Branch Lines series - see town names
Brecon to Neath D 43 2
Brecon to Newport D 16 6
Brecon to Newtown E 06 2
Brighton to Eastbourne A 16 1
Brighton to Worthing A 03 1
Bristol to Taunton D 03 6
Bromley South to Rochester B 23 7
Bromsgrove to Birmingham D 87 6
Bromsgrove to Gloucester D 73 9
Broxbourne to Cambridge F16 1
Brunel - A railtour D 74 6
Bude - Branch Line to B 29 9
Burnham to Evercreech Jn B 68 0

C

Cambridge to Ely D 55 5
Canterbury - BLs around B 58 9
Cardiff to Dowlais (Cae Harris) E 47 5
Cardiff to Pontypridd E 95 6
Cardiff to Swansea E 42 0
Carlisle to Hawick E 85 7
Carmarthen to Fishguard E 66 6
Caterham & Tattenham Corner B251
Central & Southern Spain NG E 91 8
Chard and Yeovil - BLs a C 30 7
Charing Cross to Dartford A 75 8
Charing Cross to Orpington A 96 3
Cheddar - Branch Line to B 90 9
Cheltenham to Andover C 43 7
Cheltenham to Redditch D 81 4
Chester to Birkenhead F 21 5
Chester to Rhyl E 93 2
Chester to Warrington F 40 6
Chichester to Portsmouth A 14 7
Clacton and Walton - BLs to F 04 8
Clapham Jn to Beckenham Jn B 36 7

Cleobury Mortimer - BLs a E 18 5
Clevedon & Portishead - BLs to D180
Consett to South Shields E 57 4
Cornwall Narrow Gauge D 56 2
Corris and Vale of Rheidol E 65 9
Craven Arms to Llandeilo E 35 2
Craven Arms to Wellington E 33 8
Crawley to Littlehampton A 34 5
Cromer - Branch Lines around C 26 0
Croydon to East Grinstead B 48 0
Crystal Palace & Catford Loop B 87 1
Cyprus Narrow Gauge E 13 0

D

Darjeeling Revisited F 09 3
Darlington Leamside Newcastle E 28 4
Darlington to Newcastle D 98 2
Dartford to Sittingbourne B 34 3
Denbigh - Branch Lines around F 32 1
Derwent Valley - BL to the D 06 7
Devon Narrow Gauge E 09 3
Didcot to Banbury D 02 9
Didcot to Swindon C 84 0
Didcot to Winchester C 13 0
Dorset & Somerset NG D 76 0
Douglas - Laxey - Ramsey E 75 8
Douglas to Peel C 88 8
Douglas to Port Erin C 55 0
Douglas to Ramsey D 39 5
Dover to Ramsgate A 78 9
Dublin Northwards in 1950s E 31 4
Dunstable - Branch Lines to E 27 7

E

Ealing to Slough C 42 0
Eastbourne to Hastings A 27 7
East Cornwall Mineral Railways D 22 7
East Croydon to Three Bridges A 53 6
Eastern Spain Narrow Gauge E 56 7
East Grinstead - BLs to A 07 9
East London - Branch Lines of C 44 4
East London Line B 80 0
East of Norwich - Branch Lines E 69 7
Effingham Junction - BLs a A 74 1
Ely to Norwich C 90 1
Enfield Town & Palace Gates D 32 6
Epsom to Horsham A 30 7
Eritrean Narrow Gauge E 38 3
Euston to Harrow & Wealdstone C 89 5
Exeter to Barnstaple B 15 2
Exeter to Newton Abbot C 49 9
Exeter to Tavistock B 69 5
Exmouth - Branch Lines to B 00 8

F

Fairford - Branch Line to A 52 9
Falmouth, Helston & St. Ives C 74 1
Fareham to Salisbury A 67 3
Faversham to Dover B 05 3
Felixstowe & Aldeburgh - BL to D 20 3
Fenchurch Street to Barking C 20 8
Festiniog - 50 yrs of enterprise C 83 3
Festiniog 1946-55 E 01 7
Festiniog in the Fifties B 68 8
Festiniog in the Sixties B 91 6
Ffestiniog in Colour 1955-82 F 25 3
Finsbury Park to Alexandra Pal C 02 8
Frome to Bristol B 77 0

G

Gloucester to Bristol D 35 7
Gloucester to Cardiff D 66 1
Gosport - Branch Lines around A 36 9
Greece Narrow Gauge D 72 2

H

Hampshire Narrow Gauge D 36 4
Harrow to Watford D 14 2
Harwich & Hadleigh - BLs to F 02 4

Hastings to Ashford A 37 6
Hawick to Galashiels F 36 9
Hawkhurst - Branch Line to A 66 6
Hayling - Branch Line to A 12 3
Hay-on-Wye - BL around D 92 0
Haywards Heath to Seaford A 28 4
Hemel Hempstead - BLs to D 88 3
Henley, Windsor & Marlow - BLa C77 2
Hereford to Newport D 54 8
Hertford & Hatfield - BLs a E 58 1
Hertford Loop E 71 0
Hexham to Carlisle D 75 3
Hexham to Hawick F 08 6
Hitchin to Peterborough D 07 4
Holborn Viaduct to Lewisham A 81 9
Horsham - Branch Lines to A 02 4
Huntingdon - Branch Line to A 93 2

I

Ilford to Shenfield C 97 0
Ilfracombe - Branch Line to B 21 3
Industrial Rlys of the South East A 09 3
Ipswich to Saxmundham C 41 3
Isle of Wight Lines - 50 yrs C 12 3
Italy Narrow Gauge F 17 8

K

Kent Narrow Gauge C 45 1
Kidderminster to Shrewsbury E 10 9
Kingsbridge - Branch Line to C 98 7
Kings Cross to Potters Bar E 62 8
Kingston & Hounslow Loops A 83 3
Kingswear - Branch Line to C 17 8

L

Lambourn - Branch Line to C 70 3
Launceston & Princetown - BLs C 19 2
Lewisham to Dartford A 92 5
Lines around Wimbledon B 75 6
Liverpool Street to Chingford D 01 2
Liverpool Street to Ilford C 34 5
Llandeilo to Swansea E 46 8
London Bridge to Addiscombe B 20 6
London Bridge to East Croydon A 58 1
Longmoor - Branch Lines to A 41 3
Looe - Branch Line to C 22 2
Lowestoft - BLs around E 40 6
Ludlow to Hereford E 14 7
Lydney - Branch Lines around E 26 0
Lyme Regis - Branch Line to A 45 1
Lynton - Branch Line to B 04 6

M

Machynlleth to Barmouth E 54 3
Maesteg and Tondu Lines E 06 2
Majorca & Corsica Narrow Gauge F 41 3
March - Branch Lines around B 09 1
Marylebone to Rickmansworth D 49 4
Melton Constable to Yarmouth Bch E031
Midhurst - Branch Lines of E 78 9
Midhurst - Branch Lines to F 00 0
Minehead - Branch Line to A 80 2
Mitcham Junction Lines B 01 5
Mitchell & company C 59 8
Monmouth - Branch Lines to E 20 8
Monmouthshire Eastern Valleys D 71 5
Moretonhampstead - BL to C 27 7
Moreton-in-Marsh to Worcester D 26 5
Mountain Ash to Neath D 80 7

N

Newbury to Westbury C 66 6
Newcastle to Hexham D 69 2
Newport (IOW) - Branch Lines to A 26 0
Newquay - Branch Lines to C 71 0
Newton Abbot to Plymouth C 60 4
Newtown to Aberystwyth E 41 3
North East German NG D 44 9
Northern Alpine Narrow Gauge F 37 6

Northern France Narrow Gauge C 75 8
Northern Spain Narrow Gauge E 83 3
North London Line B 94 7
North Woolwich - BLs around C 65 9
Nottingham to Lincoln F 43 7

O

Ongar - Branch Line to E 05 5
Orpington to Tonbridge B 03 9
Oswestry - Branch Lines around E 60 4
Oswestry to Whitchurch E 81 9
Oxford to Bletchley D 57 9
Oxford to Moreton-in-Marsh D 15 9

P

Paddington to Ealing C 37 6
Paddington to Princes Risborough C819
Padstow - Branch Line to B 54 1
Pembroke and Cardigan - BLs to F 29 1
Peterborough to Kings Lynne E 32 1
Plymouth - BLs around B 98 5
Plymouth to St. Austell C 63 5
Pontypool to Mountain Ash D 65 4
Pontypridd to Merthyr F 14 7
Pontypridd to Port Talbot E 86 4
Porthmadog 1954-94 - BLa B 31 2
Portmadoc 1923-46 - BLa B 13 8
Portsmouth to Southampton A 31 4
Portugal Narrow Gauge E 67 3
Potters Bar to Cambridge D 70 8
Princes Risborough - BL to D 05 0
Princes Risborough to Banbury C 85 7

R

Reading to Basingstoke B 27 5
Reading to Didcot C 79 6
Reading to Guildford A 47 5
Redhill to Ashford A 73 4
Return to Blaenau 1970-82 C 64 2
Rhyl to Bangor F 15 4
Rhymney & New Tredegar Lines E 48 2
Rickmansworth to Aylesbury D 61 6
Romania & Bulgaria NG E 23 9
Romneyrail C 32 1
Ross-on-Wye - BLs around E 30 7
Ruabon to Barmouth E 84 0
Rugby to Birmingham E 37 6
Rugby to Loughborough F 12 3
Rugby to Stafford F 07 9
Ryde to Ventnor A 19 2

S

Salisbury to Westbury B 39 8
Saxmundham to Yarmouth C 69 7
Saxony Narrow Gauge D 47 0
Seaton & Sidmouth - BLs to A 95 6
Selsey - Branch Line to A 04 8
Sheerness - Branch Line to B 16 2
Shenfield to Ipswich E 96 3
Shrewsbury - Branch Line to A 86 4
Shrewsbury to Chester E 70 3
Shrewsbury to Crewe F 48 2
Shrewsbury to Ludlow E 21 5
Shrewsbury to Newtown E 29 1
Sierra Leone Narrow Gauge D 28 9
Sirhowy Valley Line E 12 3
Sittingbourne to Ramsgate A 90 1
Slough to Newbury C 56 7
South African Two-foot gauge E 51 2
Southampton to Bournemouth A 42 0
Southend & Southminster BLs E 76 5
Southern Alpine Narrow Gauge F 22 2
Southern France Narrow Gauge C 47 5
South London Line B 46 6
South Lynn to Norwich City F 03 1
Southwold - Branch Line to A 15 4
Spalding - Branch Lines around E 52 9
Stafford to Chester F 34 5

St Albans to Bedford D 08 1
St. Austell to Penzance C 67 3
St. Boswell to Berrick F 44 4
Steaming Through Isle of Wight A 5
Steaming Through West Hants A 69
Stourbridge to Wolverhampton E 16
St. Pancras to Barking D 68 5
St. Pancras to Folkestone E 88 8
St. Pancras to St. Albans C 78 9
Stratford-u-Avon to Birmingham D7
Stratford-u-Avon to Cheltenham C2
Sudbury - Branch Lines to F 19 2
Surrey Narrow Gauge C 87 1
Sussex Narrow Gauge C 68 0
Swanley to Ashford B 45 9
Swansea - Branch Lines around F 3
Swansea to Carmarthen E 59 8
Swindon to Bristol C 96 3
Swindon to Gloucester D 46 3
Swindon to Newport D 30 2
Swiss Narrow Gauge C 94 9

T

Talyllyn 60 E 98 7
Taunton to Barnstaple B 60 2
Taunton to Exeter C 82 6
Taunton to Minehead F 39 0
Tavistock to Plymouth B 88 6
Tenterden - Branch Line to A 21 5
Three Bridges to Brighton A 35 2
Tilbury Loop C 86 4
Tiverton - BLs around C 62 8
Tivetshall to Beccles D 41 8
Tonbridge to Hastings A 44 4
Torrington - Branch Lines to B 37 4
Towcester - BLs around E 39 0
Tunbridge Wells BLs A 32 1

U

Upwell - Branch Line to B 64 0

V

Victoria to Bromley South A 98 7
Victoria to East Croydon A 40 6
Vivarais Revisited E 08 6

W

Walsall Routes F 45 1
Wantage - Branch Line to D 25 8
Wareham to Swanage 50 yrs D098
Waterloo to Windsor A 54 3
Waterloo to Woking A 38 3
Watford to Leighton Buzzard D 45 6
Welshpool to Llanfair E 49 9
Wenford Bridge to Fowey C 09 3
Westbury to Bath B 55 8
Westbury to Taunton C 76 5
West Cornwall Mineral Rlys D 48 7
West Croydon to Epsom B 08 4
West German Narrow Gauge D 93 7
West London - BLs of C 50 5
West London Line B 84 8
West Wiltshire - BLs of D 12 8
Weymouth - BLs A 65 9
Willesden Jn to Richmond B 71 8
Wimbledon to Beckenham C 58 1
Wimbledon to Epsom B 62 6
Wimborne - BLs around A 97 0
Wisbech - BLs around C 01 7
Witham & Kelvedon - BLs a E 82 6
Woking to Alton A 59 8
Woking to Portsmouth A 25 3
Woking to Southampton A 55 0
Wolverhampton to Shrewsbury E444
Worcester to Birmingham D 97 5
Worcester to Hereford D 38 8
Worthing to Chichester A 06 2
Wrexham to New Brighton F 47 5
Wroxham - BLs around F 31 4

Y

Yeovil - 50 yrs change C 38 3
Yeovil to Dorchester A 76 5
Yeovil to Exeter A 91 8
York to Scarborough F 23 9